ccjc
10/2010

Food and Cooking in Ancient Rome

Written by **Clive Gifford**
Illustrations by **Paul Cherrill**

PowerKiDS
press
New York

Published in 2010 by The Rosen Publishing Group Inc.
29 East 21st Street, New York, NY 10010

First Edition

Series Editor: Victoria Brooker
Editor: Susie Brooks
Designer: Jason Billin
Picture researcher: Shelley Noronha
Food consultant: Stella Sargeson

Library of Congress Cataloging-in-Publication Data

Gifford, Clive.
  Food and cooking in ancient Rome / Clive Gifford.
      p. cm. -- (Cooking in world cultures)
  Includes bibliographical references and index.
  ISBN 978-1-61532-339-5 (library binding)
  ISBN 978-1-61532-363-0 (paperback)
  ISBN 978-1-61532-364-7 (6-pack)
  1. Diet--Rome--Juvenile literature. 2. Cookery, Roman--Juvenile
literature. 3. Food habits--Rome--Juvenile literature. I. Title.
  TX360.R64G54 2010
  394.1'20945632--dc22

                              2009024202

Photographs:
cover and 6 akg-images/Gilles Mermet; 4 Peter Bull; 5, 7, 10, 14,
17 akg-images/Erich Lessing; 8 Werner Forman Archive; 9 Musee
des Antiquites Nationales, St. Germain-en-Laye,
France/Lauros/Giraudon/The Bridgeman Art Library;12, 28 akg-
images/Bildarchiv Steffens; 16 Musee des Antiquites Nationales,
St. Germain-en-Laye, France/Lauros/Giraudon/The Bridgeman
Art Library; 18 Museo della Civilta Romana, Rome, Italy/Roger-
Viollet, Paris/The Bridgeman Art Library; 20 © Layne
Kennedy/CORBIS; 21 The Art Archive/Gianni Dagli Orti;
22: The Art Archive/Gianni Dagli Orti; 24 The Art Archive/
Bardo Museum Tunis/Gianni Dagli Orti; 26 The Art Archive/
Museo Prenestino Palestrina/Alfredo Dagli Orti/Gianni Dagli
Orti; 27 The Art Archive/Bardo Museum Tunis/Gianni Dagli
Orti; 29 © Werner Forman/CORBIS

Manufactured in China

CPSIA Compliance Information: Batch #WAW0102PK: For Further Information

contact Rosen Publishing, New York, New York at 1-800-237-9932

Contents

A mighty Empire 4

Farms and estates 6

Bread and bakeries 8

Fruit and vegetables 10

Roman kitchens 12

Daily dining 14

Dinner time! 16

Off to market 18

Roman sauces 20

Eating out 22

Honoring the gods 24

A Roman banquet 26

The Romans in Britain 28

Glossary 30

Further Information and Web Sites 31

Index 32

A mighty Empire

In the eighth century BCE, a small village named Rome grew up near the River Tiber in central Italy. Soon to become a mighty city, it formed the center of the ancient Roman civilization. The Romans conquered many lands and had a series of powerful leaders. Their civilization thrived for over 1,000 years.

Growing power

Until 509 BCE, Rome was ruled by foreign kings. Then it became a **republic**, lasting for 500 years. During this time, the Romans took over much of Italy before seizing lands around the Mediterranean and into Northern Europe. They built spectacular straight roads, making it easy for their skilled army to reach its targets and attack.

The **Roman Empire** began in 27 BCE, when Emperor Augustus was crowned. Under his, and his successors', power, the civilization grew and grew.

▶ *The Roman Empire at its largest included large parts of Europe and the entire coastline surrounding the Mediterranean Sea.*

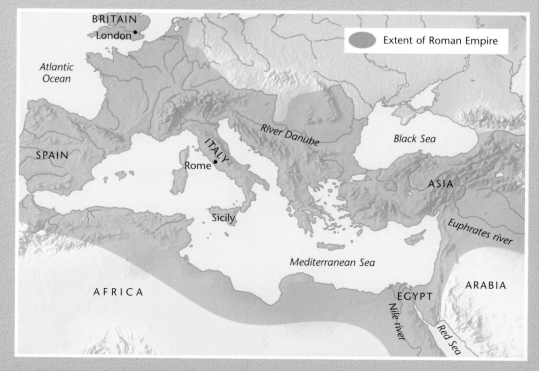

Extent of Roman Empire

BRITAIN
London

Atlantic Ocean

SPAIN

ITALY
Rome

River Danube

Black Sea

ASIA

Euphrates river

Sicily

Mediterranean Sea

ARABIA

AFRICA

EGYPT

Nile river

Red Sea

Recipe for success

Millions of people under the Romans' rule took on Roman dress, customs, and ways of living. Yet the Romans also borrowed elements of other peoples' lifestyles for their own use—including ideas for cooking. The many different lands and peoples drawn into the Roman Empire provided rich and varied sources of food, from European cattle to grain from Egypt.

Lasting taste

The Roman Empire eventually collapsed with invasions by Germanic peoples in the late fifth century CE. But it was not forgotten. Even today, we have the Romans to thank for important developments in engineering, law, transportation, trade, and culture. Their legacy includes central heating and the written alphabet. It was the Romans who set up the huge wine industries in France, Spain, and Italy. They also began the tradition of serving three-course meals.

▲ *Roman traders and sailors load a ship with birds and plants for transportation by sea.*

Farms and estates

Roman farms came in a range of different sizes. The tiniest **small-holdings** grew barely enough to feed a family, while giant estates produced huge amounts of food for trade.

Crops and creatures

The Romans grew a variety of cereal crops, including barley and wheat, and many types of vegetable. They kept sheep, pigs, and birds such as chickens, ducks, and pigeons. Some larger Roman farms had ponds for rearing fish and some freshwater shellfish.

All kinds of skills

A mixture of skills helped the Romans to be great farmers. They developed existing technology, such as plows and **irrigation** systems, to make crop-growing more efficient. They also understood the soil, adding animal manure as a fertilizer to enrich it. Fruits were grown in sophisticated orchards, and large vineyards produced grapes to make the Romans' favorite drink—wine.

► *This mosaic picture made up of small ceramic tiles shows a farmer using two oxen to plow a field while a farmhand sows seed.*

Living off the land

Many soldiers in the Roman army were rewarded with a small plot of land when they retired. They could grow food and sell it to active soldiers at good rates. Other small farmers were not so lucky and sometimes struggled to grow enough to eat. To boost their diet, they hunted wild animals such as deer, wild boar, pigeons, partridges, and rabbits. They also gathered wild fruits and plants—nettles, for example, were used in salads and boiled to make a tealike drink.

▼ *The lands around a large country villa provided the wealthy villa owner with much food.*

Luxury estates

By around 100 BCE, many small farms had been taken over by wealthy Romans to form large estates. The landowners had luxurious villas built, yet they often lived in towns or cities for much of the year. Staff ran the estate in the owner's absence. A *vilicus*, for instance, was the manager who supervised farm work. As the Roman Empire flourished, most people working on farms were slaves.

The first combine harvester

Cereal crops were harvested entirely by hand until the invention of the *vallus*. This early reaping or harvesting machine consisted of a cart with a row of teeth at the front. Pushed along by a bull or donkey, it cut the wheat and collected it in the cart.

Bread and bakeries

In the early Roman years, farmers grew a form of husked wheat called *far*. This was turned into a thick, filling porridge that tasted very bland. Centuries later, bread made from cereal crops, such as wheat, barley, and rye, became the most important part of the diet of ordinary Romans.

Crushing the crop

It took a lot of work to turn a cereal crop into bread. After harvesting, the crop had to be threshed to separate the grain from the straw. Many farmers drove horses across the crop to do this. Then the grain was taken in sacks to a mill, where it was ground between large stones to make flour.

Mills and bakeries

The Romans developed larger mills than anyone before. At first, the machinery was powered by slaves or donkeys, then waterwheels were used. Many towns had a bakery, called a *pistrinum*, that milled its own flour and baked bread in brick ovens for sale. **Excavations** of Pompeii have revealed 33 bakeries in that city alone.

◀ *The remains of a flour mill at Pompeii, show giant grindstones built into the floor.*

Rich bread, poor bread

The Romans used many forms of flour to make different types of bread. Cheap, dark flour made gritty black bread—the only type the poor could afford. Whiter flour, and breads made with spices, nuts, seeds, or honey, were more expensive. When the Emperor Trajan came to power in 98 CE, he made it a custom to distribute free bread every day to the poorest people of Rome.

Bread for all courses

Bread was eaten with most meals and was a major part of soldiers' rations. People dipped it in oil or wine or ate it with pastes and cheese. The Romans also made a simple dessert by breaking the crust of loaves into large pieces. These were soaked in milk, fried in hot oil, and served with honey poured over them.

▲ *A Roman baker places bread into a hot oven in this mosaic.*

The Barbegal mills

The Barbegal mills were built around 300 BCE in southern France, and were powered by 16 large waterwheels. Historians think that these mills could have created 4 tons of flour a day—enough to bake bread for up to 80,000 people.

Fruit and vegetables

Rich Romans ate a lot of fresh fruit and vegetables. Many country villas had their own market gardens, orchards, and vineyards.

Vegetable patch

The Romans grew a wide range of vegetables including cabbages, turnips, broccoli, endives, radishes, leeks, lentils, broad beans, peas, and lettuces. Often, these were tougher than the types grown today, so the Romans mashed, boiled, or fried them to soften them.

Fruity favorites

In large Roman towns and cities, grapes and olives were highly prized. Olives grew in the Mediterranean regions and were eaten whole, or pressed to make olive oil. Grapes were eaten fresh, dried into raisins, crushed to make grape juice, or **fermented** for wine. Other popular fruits included peaches, plums, figs, and melons.

▲ *This mosaic shows workers picking grapes from vines.*

Growing new trees

The Romans became highly skilled and experienced fruit growers. They learned how to take cuttings from vines and olive trees to grow new plants. They also began to graft fruit trees—attaching the twigs of one tree to the branch of another in an attempt to improve the quality and amount of fruit.

Stuffed dates

The Romans loved dates, especially when they were stuffed or soaked in wine. This recipe is based on *Dulcia Domestica*, meaning "homemade dessert," from a Roman cookbook called *Apicius*.

Serves 4

You will need:
1⅓ cup (200g) dates
¼ cup (30g) almonds
¼ cup (30g) hazelnuts

1 teaspoon cinnamon
½ cup (100ml) red grape juice
3½ tablespoons (50ml) honey
Dish of salt or sea salt

1. Carefully slice the dates along one side and remove the stone.

2. Crush or chop the nuts very roughly so they are in halves or quarters. Sprinkle the pieces with cinnamon.

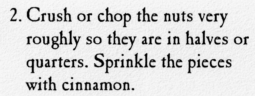

3. Stuff the dates with the nut mixture and squeeze the slit shut. Roll them in the salt a little.

4. Warm the honey and grape juice in a pan, then put in the dates. Warm them on low heat for around 7–8 minutes.

5. Put the dates onto a plate and serve.

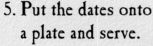

Roman kitchens

Roman kitchens varied greatly according to a person's wealth or importance. Poor people often had no kitchen at all—just a bare fire for cooking if they were lucky. Merchants and landowners had large, well-equipped kitchens, with slaves to prepare and cook meals.

Ovens galore

In a Roman villa, the kitchen had everything a chef might need. A fire in a stone or brick hearth provided heat to boil, fry, and stew foods. Sometimes, a **spit** was built above it to roast whole animals or large joints. Baking was done in a stone oven, often with a clay dome inside to cover the food.

Cooking tools

The Romans cooked with many of the basic kitchen tools we use today, from sieves and ladles, to chopping boards and baking sheets. Pots and pans were made of iron or bronze and were often placed on metal tripods above a fire. A large kitchen would have a number of different-height **tripods**, so the pot could be placed nearer or farther away from the flames.

▼ *An ancient kitchen features a shelf of pottery jars to store ingredients, an oven, and a brazier.*

Roman lamb stew

Meat was expensive in Roman times, but wealthy villa owners still ate plenty of it. This stew can be served with vegetables and a hunk of fresh bread.

Serves 4

You will need:

2 tablespoons olive oil
1⅓ lb. (600g) lean lamb, cut into
  1 in. (2.5cm) cubes
3 garlic cloves, crushed
1 medium onion
½ teaspoon ground cumin

1 teaspoon coriander seeds
1 teaspoon celery seeds or handful of
  celery leaves
2 teaspoons Nam Pla (Vietnamese fish sauce)
¾ cup (180ml) red grape juice
1½ tablespoons (20ml) vinegar
1 tablespoon cornflour

1. Heat half of the oil in a large pan. Add the lamb and crushed garlic, and keep stirring until the cubes turn brown on all sides.

2. Chop the onion as finely as possible and then crush the onion with the cumin, coriander seeds, and celery.

3. Mix the rest of the olive oil, the fish sauce, and the grape juice and vinegar together with the onion and herbs. Pour this over the meat in the pan.

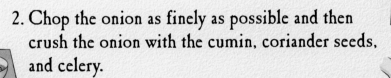

4. Let the pan simmer gently for at least 1½ hours.

5. Mix the cornflour with a little water in a jug and then pour it in to thicken the stew juices. Bring the stew to the boil, then take off the heat, ready to serve.

Daily dining

The Romans usually ate three meals a day. The meals started small and ended with a big dinner.

Simple start

Breakfast, known as *ientaculum*, was a simple meal. Most Romans ate porridge or flat, round loaves of bread dipped in olive oil, water, or wine. Cheese, olives, and raisins would often be sprinkled on top.

Light lunch

Prandium (lunch) was usually served cold. Along with bread, there were cold meats, fruit, and any leftovers from dinner the night before. Cheese was a popular part of Roman lunches and was made from the milk of cows, goats, or sometimes sheep. By the time of the Roman Empire, there were dozens of different cheeses available, if you were wealthy enough to afford them.

Mortarium mush

The Romans liked to pulp many foods into pastes, dips, and sauces. They would pound seeds, spices, herbs, and some vegetables in a heavy bowl called a *mortarium*, using a stone rod or ball. This was similar to the mortar and pestle used by chefs today.

▼ *This stone relief shows Romans in their best clothes sharing a meal.*

Mixtura cum caseo

This leek, lettuce, and cheese paste was used as a dip for bread and vegetables.

Serves 4

You will need:

1 medium leek
1 small, crunchy lettuce, chopped
1 handful arugula leaves
1 handful fresh cilantro and parsley, chopped
4 mint leaves

2 tablespoons white wine vinegar
1¾ oz. (50g) parmesan cheese
7 oz. (200g) feta cheese
3 tablespoons olive oil
½ teaspoon ground black pepper

1. Cut the leek into thin ½-in.-wide (1cm-wide) strips. Boil in a pan of water until soft.

2. Drain the leeks and place in a blender or food processor. Add the lettuce, arugula, herbs, and vinegar.

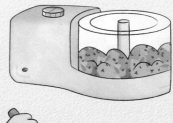

3. Grate the parmesan and crumble the feta and add these to the blender.

4. Switch the blender on and process until all the ingredients form a smooth paste.

5. Place the mixture in a bowl and mix in the olive oil and pepper thoroughly.

6. Eat with warm bread or crunchy vegetables, such as carrot and cucumber sticks.

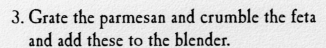

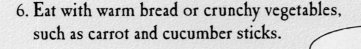

Dinner time!

The Romans looked forward to dinner, or *cena*. This main meal was eaten in the late afternoon. Poor households made do with bread, porridge, vegetables, and any meat they could find. The wealthy, meanwhile, feasted on three courses.

In the triclinium

In a wealthy person's villa or townhouse, *cena* was served in the *triclinium*. This grand dining room was decorated with **mosaics** and **tapestries**, with torches or oil lamps for light. Low-lying couches were placed around a table so that male guests could recline, eat, and drink. Until the later Roman years, women had to perch on the edge of the couch.

▲ Romans recline and eat dinner (left) while a servant (right) brings another course.

On the menu

The first course, or *gustatio*, was a tempting spread of appetizers such as shellfish, egg dishes, and salad. This was followed by the *fercula* (main course) of meat and fish, sometimes with vegetables and sauces. Instead of clearing the table before dessert, servants would remove it and bring in a new table full of fruit, nuts, and cake. The meal was washed down with a selection of wines.

Table manners

Before they sat, diners removed their sandals, and slaves washed the diners' feet and hands. The Romans ate mainly with their fingertips, dipping them in water scented with flower petals between courses. Guests used napkins called *mappae*, sometimes bringing their own to wrap up leftovers to take home. Any unwanted scraps, such as bones or shells, were thrown to the floor for the servants to sweep up. Belching was considered not only polite but praise for the food on offer.

Table tools

The Romans sometimes used iron-bladed knives to cut foods into smaller pieces. For runny dishes, they had spoons made from bone, bronze, or silver. One type of spoon, called a *cochlear*, had a spike or pointed handle at one end. This was used for teasing and poking shellfish and snails from their shells.

▼ *This is the interior of a Roman house with its walls richly decorated with mosaics.*

Off to market

In the Roman Empire, food was always on the move. It was transported from region to region by ship or wagon, ready to be traded with anyone willing to pay. Much food shopping took place in the market square, or **forum**, of Roman towns and cities.

Sellers and stalls

The forum was surrounded on three sides by covered walkways. These contained craft shops, butcher shops, and bakeries with open fronts. Other food stalls were pitched in the open square. They sold all manner of goods from olive oil and wine, stored in clay jars called *amphorae*, to herbs and spices. Rare delicacies, such as small birds and wild mushrooms, were also on offer.

Lively landmark

The forum became the focus of everyday life in Roman towns and cities. People would meet there to chat or for public or political meetings. Jugglers and other entertainers would try to earn a living in the forum, and hot-food sellers offered their wares to hungry shoppers.

▼ *This stone relief shows a butcher (right) at work in his small shop producing cuts of meat.*

Trajan's Forum

The Emperor Trajan, who ruled from 98 to 117 CE, ordered the building of a giant forum in Rome. Trajan's Forum, the size of a couple of football fields, was home to hundreds of shops and stalls selling oil, wine, seafood, and vegetables.

Honey and spinach omelette

This simple dish is great as a quick snack food.

Serves 2

You will need:

½ cup (50g) fresh spinach leaves   ¼ cup (50ml) milk
1 tablespoon (15ml) olive oil   3½ tablespoons (50ml) honey
4 large eggs   Black pepper

1. Tear the spinach leaves into pieces and place in a hot pan with a sprinkle of water. Cook for 1 minute until the leaves begin to soften. Remove from the pan.

2. Beat the eggs and milk together.

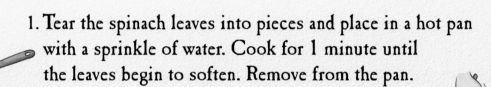

3. Heat the oil in the pan and pour in the mixture. Add the spinach. Keep this cooking over low heat.

4. Warm the honey in a small pan. Don't let it boil.

5. When the omelette is cooked through, take it off the heat and lift it out onto a plate. Pour the warmed honey on the omelette and grind a little pepper over the top.

Serve immediately.

Roman sauces

Roman food was often packed with very strong flavors! Cooks would sometimes use a large range of herbs, spices, and other ingredients to create these flavors.

Strong smells

Why were the Romans so fond of highly flavored foods? One theory is that foods spoiled as they traveled around the Empire, so strong spices and herbs were used to disguise nasty tastes and smells. Other people think that Romans living in cities may have suffered from lead poisoning, because their drinking water ran through lead pipes. Lead poisoning can dull your sense of taste, creating a need to spice things up.

Ancient flavors

The Romans used garlic, onion, and soured wine or vinegar in many dishes. They also prized strong-flavored herbs including lovage, pennyroyal, dill, and silphium—a powerful-tasting relative of fennel that grew in Libya and is now thought to be **extinct**.

▲ *The bright yellow flowers of a lovage plant. The stem, leaves, and seeds of a lovage plant were all used by the Romans as flavoring in many dishes.*

Super-sauces

Garum and *liquamen* (see page 21) were so often used in Roman meals that the ruins of large sauce factories have been found in Italy, Portugal, and Spain. Some Romans even used the sauces as medicine, thought to cure many ills, from **dysentery** to dog bites!

Fizzy fish

Two fish sauces, *garum* and *liquamen*, were extremely popular—and pungent. Historians believe that *garum* was lumpy, but *liquamen* was strained and was thinner. Some fish sauces were made from the entrails (innards) of fish, mixed with salt or left to ferment, so they started to bubble and fizz.

Keeping sweet

The Romans had no sugar—but honey, fruit, and fruit juices did a similar job. Some delicate dishes were even sweetened using flower petals. More frequently, wine or grapes were boiled down to create a sweet **must** called *caroenum*. If this was boiled for a lot longer and mixed with honey, it formed a thick, sickly syrup known as *passum*. The Romans particularly enjoyed sweet and sour tastes, so would sometimes mix vinegar or *liquamen* with *passum* or honey as a sauce for meats and vegetables.

▼ *These broken jars were used to make* garum *in the Roman trading post of Tipasa on the northern coast of Africa.*

Eating out

In Rome and other large cities, a full kitchen was a luxury that few people could afford. Many city dwellers lived in cramped apartments or flimsy wooden housing, where lighting fires was banned. Eating out was an everyday habit for many Romans, especially travelers and those living in large towns.

Ancient eateries

Street stalls and shops sold endless hot foods, from sausages to stews and pastries filled with nuts and fruit. **Taverns** were found in towns and at crossroads in the countryside. A *thermopolium* was a tavern that served wine mixed with hot water, and foods such as spicy meats, *isicia* (meat patties), cheese, and olives.

Mobile meals

Many people traveled around the Roman Empire on its excellent roads, either on horseback, in a wagon or cart, or by foot. They often carried food such as hard breads and crackers, figs, and hunks of meat. On long journeys, they might also gather wild plants, catch a hare or bird, or buy foods from roadside stalls.

▼ *The thermopolium at the Roman city of Pompeii sold hot food and warmed wine. These were served in **earthenware** jars, sunk into the bar counter.*

Isicia omentata

This ground beef dish, a little like a modern hamburger, could be bought from street sellers.

Makes 10–14

You will need:

1 large hamburger bun
⅞ cup (200ml) white grape juice
3 teaspoons vinegar

1 lb. 2 oz. (500g) lean ground beef
⅜ cup (75g) pine kernels, crushed or finely chopped
3 teaspoons Nam Pla (Vietnamese fish sauce)
½ teaspoon freshly ground pepper

1. Tear up the hamburger bun into small pieces and let it soak in a dish with around half of the grape juice and all of the vinegar.

2. Heat the remaining grape juice in a pan and boil until it has reduced to half the amount. It should be sticky and syrupy.

3. Mix the meat with the bread and pine kernels thoroughly. Sprinkle the Nam Pla and pepper evenly through the mixture and stir it in.

4. Form the mixture into small burger shapes. Line a shallow dish or tray with baking foil and spoon in some of the sticky grape juice.

5. Place the burgers on top and broil for about 4–5 minutes on each side, until they are cooked thoroughly. Serve in a bun or with salad.

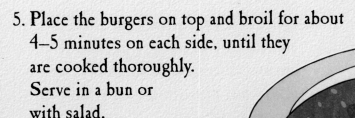

Honoring the gods

The Romans worshiped a variety of gods, many of which were borrowed from the ancient Greeks and renamed. Some gods were honored in people's homes, and others had dedicated temples and festivals.

Gods of all

The three most important Roman gods were Jupiter, who ruled the sky; Juno, the goddess of women; and Minerva, protector of soldiers and children. The *lares familiares* were less powerful guardian spirits that looked after the health and wealth of a household. Many Roman homes had a small **shrine**, called a *lararium*, where the family made offerings of food, wine, and flowers to keep the spirits happy.

▲ *A mosaic depicting the goddess Ceres harvesting wheat.*

Farming and festivals

The chief god of agriculture was Ceres, renamed from the Greek goddess, Demeter. From Ceres, we get the word "cereal," and she guarded over good harvests and crops. The Romans held many festivals around planting and harvesting times. They danced, feasted, and sacrificed animals to please the gods.

Saturnalia

Saturnalia was the biggest winter festival, held in mid-December. Sacrifices were made at the temple of Saturn, the god of farming, and festivities continued with games, feasting, and gifts. Many slave owners switched roles with their slaves for a day as part of the festival.

Libum

Libum was a type of honeyed cake, often used as an offering to household gods and spirits. This is a modern-day version of the recipe.

Serves 2–4

You will need:

¾ cup (175ml) honey, in a jar
2 whole bay leaves
a few fresh oregano leaves

1¼ cup (120g) all-purpose flour
1 egg
½ lb. (225g) drained ricotta cheese

1–2 WEEKS IN ADVANCE
Place the whole herbs into the jar of honey, screw on the lid, and store in a cool place. When you're ready to cook, remove the herbs.

1. Heat the oven to 425°F (220°C). Place the flour in a bowl and add the egg. Carefully whisk these together.

2. Beat the ricotta cheese until it is soft, then mix it into the flour to form a dough.

3. Divide the dough into four bun shapes and place on a greased baking sheet. Place a large ovenproof dish over the buns and bake for 35 minutes until firm.

4. Near the end of the baking time, pour the honey into an ovenproof dish and gently warm it.

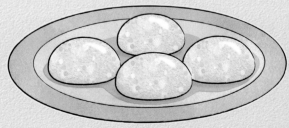

5. Take the buns out of the oven and prick all over with a fork, then place in the dish of honey and spoon it over them. Leave for 20–30 minutes so that the buns soak up most of the honey, turning them halfway. Serve immediately.

A Roman banquet

Wealthy Romans enjoyed many fine dinners in their luxurious homes, but a banquet was something to get excited about. A full banquet could see guests gorge themselves on eight, nine, or more courses. Some marathon banquets lasted up to ten hours.

Far-flung flavors

Many exotic and rare foods were eaten at the most lavish banquets. Chefs fattened snails and dormice in advance by feeding them with milk. Some people went out of their way to get foods from the edges of the Empire, such as English oysters, rare **truffles,** and asparagus stored in the ice and snow of the Alps. Lucky Emperors got an early form of ice cream, made of snow mixed with sweet wine, flour, and honey.

Hosts often tried to outdo each other for the most outrageous dishes. Whole newborn rabbits were in fashion for a time, as were flamingo tongues, peacock brains, ostrich, and even elephant's trunk. Some people placed pearls, amber, or slivers of gold among their dishes.

▲ *Wealthy Romans recline at a banquet on couches covered in cloth. A musician stands close to the banquet guests, playing a stringed instrument called a lyre.*

Not for the squeamish

Banquets were sometimes hard to stomach if you were squeamish. For example, a goatfish might be brought to the table still alive because it turned a dazzling red when it died out of the water. Some banquets included a *porcus Troianus*, or Trojan pig. This was a whole pig, stuffed with Roman sausages and fruit and roasted. When the animal was cut open, the sausages would spill out like its guts.

Party pieces

Entertainment was provided at large banquets by musicians, clowns, acrobats, dancers, and occasionally, magicians. The works of great poets might also be read, as talk and debate echoed around the room and the wine kept flowing. Some guests tried to be careful about what they discussed for fear of spies and plots.

Sub rosa

At many Roman banquets, a rose was hung from the ceiling or rose petals sprinkled down. This was partly to remind guests that anything said at the gathering was *sub rosa*, meaning it should remain secret.

▼ *Romans eat from bowls on low-lying tables using spoons in this mosaic scene discovered in Carthage, Tunisia.*

The Romans in Britain

The Romans made several attempts at invading Britain, but it wasn't until 43 CE that they began to have success. By 78 CE, they had captured much of England and Wales from the ruling **Celts**. Their power lasted for almost 350 years.

New towns

The Romans made their mark throughout Britain. Towns like Cirencester, Silchester, and Winchester were built in Roman styles, complete with Roman forums and churches. New trading settlements, called *vicus*, sprang up, too. All these places needed to be supplied with food, and this had a big impact on British farming.

Flourishing farms

The Celts had grown cereal crops, gathered wild plants and animals, and reared cattle, sheep, and pigs. With the Romans came new roads and greater use of river transportation, making it possible for farmers to transport and sell their food far and wide. Farms grew in number and size, and farmers began planting a much wider variety of crops.

▼ *The Roman fort of Portchester was built on England's south coast in the third century CE.*

Roman greens

The Romans introduced many new vegetables, such as onions, lettuce, lentils, leeks, and celery, which are still grown in Britain today. They also planted herbs, including dill, garlic, fennel, sage, and rosemary; new fruits such as plums, apples, and damsons; and walnut and sweet chestnut trees. Mediterranean favorites such as olives and figs were imported in ships, because they did not grow well in Britain's cool, wet climate.

Local livestock

The Romans did enjoy some of the food available in Britain, particularly beef and pork. They kept pigs in sties to help fatten them up. They also fenced off areas of land as game parks where deer, pheasants, wild boar, and other animals could be hunted.

Cockles and mussels

The Celts only bothered with shellfish when there were food shortages. But to the Romans, oysters and other shellfish were a great delicacy. Around parts of the coast, large industries grew up catching and preparing oysters, cockles, and mussels. In one Roman site near Silchester, over one million oyster shells were found.

◀ *In Roman times, wild boar used to live in Britain's forests. This mosaic shows a boar being hunted by two men using a spear and hunting dogs.*

Glossary

Celts peoples who lived in the British Isles, Northern France, and other parts of Europe who the Romans conquered as they extended their territory.

earthenware a type of pottery made of clay.

excavation to dig down or to clear away loose soil and sand, to try to uncover ancient buildings or objects.

extinct a species of plant or animal that no longer exists on Earth.

dysentery a disease of the digestive system usually caused by unclean water containing bacteria.

ferment types of chemical reactions including ways of converting sugar in foods into alcohol.

fertile when used about land, it means that the soil and conditions are good for growing crops.

forum a place for meeting or conducting official business, which in Roman times was usually in a city or town square.

irrigation a system of channels that supply an area of land with water, particularly to allow crops to grow well.

mosaic a picture or decorative design made by setting small colored pieces of stone, or tile, into a surface.

must a thick, sticky sweet syrup often made in Roman times by boiling down wine or grape juice.

preserve ways to keep food from spoiling so that it can be eaten at a later date.

republic a way of governing a country with elected representatives and no king or queen as head of state.

Roman Empire the political system that succeeded the Roman Republic in around 27 BCE and lasted almost five centuries.

small-holding a small piece of land that is used to grow crops or rear animals on.

spit a long spike on which meat was speared and then roasted over an open fire.

tapestries cloth woven with designs or scenes which were frequently hung on walls for decoration.

tavern a type of inn or place to stay for travelers that sold food and often alcoholic drinks.

tripod a three-legged stand for a cooking pot.

truffles types of edible fungi that grow near tree roots and are prized as a delicacy.

villa the name given to a large country house lived in by wealthy Romans.

Further Information and Web Sites

Books

Exploring Ancient Civilizations: Rome by Tracey Ann Schofield
(Teaching and Learning Co, 2002)

Roman Cookery by Jane Renfew (English Heritage, 2005)

Roman Cookery: Ancient Recipes For Modern Kitchens by Mark Grant
(Interlink Publishing, 2008)

The Romans: Life in Ancient Rome by Liz Sonneborn (Millbrook Press, 2009)

Web Sites

Due to the changing nature of Internet links, PowerKids Press has developed an online list of Web sites related to the subject of this book. This site is updated regularly. Please use this link to access this list:
http://www.powerkidslinks.com/ciwc/rome/

Index

Augustus, Emperor 4

bakers 9, 18
bakery 8–9, 9
banquet 26–27, 26
birds 5, 6, 18, 22
bread 8–9, 9, 13, 14, 15, 16,
  22, 23
breakfast 14
Britain 28–29
butcher 18, 18

cake 16
cattle 5
Celts 28, 29
cereal 6, 7, 8, 24, 28
cheese 9, 14, 15, 22, 25
cooking 5, 12
crops 6, 7, 8, 24, 28

dining room 16, 16
dinner 14, 16–17, 16, 26

eggs 16, 19, 25
Egypt 4, 5
estate 6–7

farmers 6, 6, 7, 8
farms 6–7, 28
fertilizer 6
fish 6, 16, 21, 23, 27
flour 8, 9
forum 18, 28
France 4, 5
fruit 6, 7, 10–11, 16, 19, 22, 29

garlic 13, 20
gods 24, 24, 25
grapes 6, 10, 10, 21

harvest 7, 8, 24
herbs 14, 15, 18, 20, 20, 25, 29
honey 9, 11, 19, 21, 25, 26
hunting 29, 29

irrigation 6
Italy 4, 5, 20

kitchen 12–13, 12, 22

lunch 14

market 18–19
meals 5, 9, 12, 14, 14, 16–17
meat 6, 7, 12, 13, 13, 14, 16,
  18, 21, 22, 23, 27, 29
medicine 20
milk 9, 14, 19, 26
mills 8, 8, 9
mosaic 6, 9, 10, 16, 17, 24,
  27, 29

nuts 9, 11, 11, 16, 22, 29

oil 9, 10, 13, 14, 15, 18, 19
olives 10, 14, 22, 29
oven 8, 9, 12, 12

paste 9, 14, 15, 15
plants 5, 7, 10, 22, 28
plow 6
Pompeii 8, 8, 22

raisins 10, 14
ration 9
recipes
  honey and spinach omelette 19
  isicia omentata 23
  libum 25
  mixtura cum caseo 15

Roman lamb stew 13
  stuffed dates 11
republic 4
Roman Empire 4, 4, 5, 7, 14,
  18, 22
Rome 4, 22

sauces 14, 16, 20–21, 23
shellfish 6, 16, 17, 26, 29
shops 18, 22
slaves 7, 12, 16, 17, 24
soldiers 7, 9, 24
Spain 4, 5, 20
spices 9, 11, 13, 14, 18, 20
stalls 18, 22

tavern 22, 22
tools 12, 17, 27
trade 5, 5, 6, 18, 28, 29
Trajan, Emperor 9, 18
tripod 12
truffles 26

utensils see tools

vallus 7
vegetables 6, 10, 13, 14, 15, 15,
  16, 18, 19, 21, 26, 29
villa 7, 7, 10, 16
vinegar 15, 20, 23
vineyard 6, 10, 10

water 14, 17, 20, 22
wine 5, 6, 9, 10, 13, 14, 16, 18,
  20, 21, 22, 24, 26, 27